MW01535396

MGFL!

Much Girlfriend Love

By Jo Ann Darby

Nuggets of Encouragement for the Girlfriend's Heart and Soul.

WP   Published by Warren Publishing, Inc.
Cornelius, NC
www.warrenpublishing.net

The opinions expressed in this book are solely the opinions of the author
and in no way constitute an official endorsement of any product or service.

Text copyright © 2011 Jo Ann Darby

Published by Warren Publishing, Inc.

All rights reserved. No part of this book may be reproduced or transmitted
in any form by any means, electronic or mechanical, including photocopying,
recording, or by any information storage system, without permission in
writing from the Publisher.

www.warrenpublishing.net

ISBN 978-1-886057-65-4
Library of Congress Catalog Number : 2011936311
Manufactured in the United States of America

First Edition

17039 Kenton Drive, 101-B,
Cornelius, NC 28031

Dedication

It's all HIS, it's all from HIM, it's all about HIM!

HIS words to me on the way to pick my kids up from school one day were, "Jo Ann, MGFL! My Gift Forever Lives!" And I said back to Him, "MGFL! My God Forever Loves!"

Every word was inspired FROM HIM…so HE is the ONLY one to whom this book could possibly be dedicated.

My Charity of Choice

DH DOUBLEHARVEST†
SOWING SEEDS OF LIFE

Double Harvest – Haiti
Tom Van Wingerden Memorial Fund
55 South Main Street
Oberlin, OH 44074
www.DoubleHarvest.org
440-714-1694

"Sow Seeds of Life"
in an impoverished situation

MGFL!
Mission

The girlfriend movement is designed to motivate,
encourage and uplift women by providing everyday
advice for the extraordinary woman! Words of
guidance to provide support, strength, understanding
and endurance to overcome the challenges of life.
A sisterhood movement uniting women of all races
and ages. Thus, inspiring a renewed confidence that
propels each other in a positive direction.
MGFL...Much Girlfriend Love!

Introduction

I started writing The Girlfriend Book II as soon as the original Girlfriend Book headed off to press!

As I wrote my thoughts and posted these thoughts on Facebook, I quickly realized I was working on two books simultaneously!

I found myself posting more of the motivational tips and receiving comments, inbox messages & emails with regard to these comments. It became very clear to me that these were two very different books.

I would sign off on all my comments online and also when autographing my first book with the words "Much Girlfriend Love...MGFL!" In a moment of inspiration, it became clear to me that this book was to be called "Much Girlfriend Love...MGFL!" not "The Girlfriend Book II."

The nuggets of inspiration and motivation included in this book, came to me early each morning, starting in June 2010 and continuing through January 2011. I couldn't WAIT to wake up and hurry downstairs in my home and spend quiet time meditating on what to blog/post on Facebook.

Soon, people started coming up to me in pubic and commenting on how the post of the day was just the thing they needed to hear! I told them " I ONLY post/blog what I need to tell MYSELF!" Their remarks were "That's why we love you, Jo Ann!" Their comments encouraged ME to keep pushing forward to bring you the enclosed treasure.

Actually, while compiling this book, I was going through one of the most painful years of my life! That is why you will FEEL every comment in this book as you read it!

Every single one of these statements is included for a reason, a pull, a purpose! If you bought this book or it was given to you as a gift, I believe with ALL MY HEART there is a reason it is in your hands!!! I truly believe it was DIVINE intervention!

"Sometimes ya gotta go to that place to get to this one!" Well sunshine, we are now connected deeply! So WHOEVER you are out there who needed Much Girlfriend Love...MGFL!...YOU have been ALL worth it!!!

Warm regards,
Jo Ann Darby

Much Girlfriend Love..."MGFL!"

*We would love to hear YOUR story! Especially, if this book has made a difference in your life! You just might be included as part of the next Girlfriend Book in this ongoing series! Email me at **Info@thegirlfriendbook.com**

It seems that sooner or later everyone deals with some type of great distress in their lives. Overcoming these ordeals makes you stronger, more able, and more relatable to guide someone else facing the same issues. Making a difference in the lives of others is one of life's greatest fulfillments!

There are times in your life (unfortunately) when you have to go through a cleansing process. It's hard to go through it but it purifies you! During this phase (yes, phase because it won't last forever) a deeper understanding of yourself and your situation is revealed. You become stronger as a result. When you are in one of these times, choose to learn and be open to a reshaping of your life. Realize you WILL be better as a result! When you are not in one of those times, be thankful and reflect on the lessons you learned when you were. Continue to apply them and continue to move forward!

Didn't expect to be at this point in your life where you are now? Can't believe THIS is your life? Things aren't what you planned? Everyone has a journey, everyone's path curves differently. But remember ... everyone's trail has branches to bend, thorns to watch out for, objects to step over, hills to climb and rivers to cross! No one has been down your path and you haven't been down their path!

Until someone has walked in your shoes, lived in your world, and dealt with your challenges they CAN'T judge or condemn you! Stop caring what they think, dear! Don't forget how far you've come, where you came from and what you've endured to get where you are!

Be compassionate because you might not fully grasp what someone is facing... Hopefully they will do the same for you! Let's encourage one another! Sometimes the path we are headed down wasn't what we expected but if we are looking for the larger picture, the ultimate purpose, the greater scheme, the completeness of our lives surfaces – even when we really don't understand it all and it doesn't seem fair!

Live each day for its own value. Take charge of your destiny by looking UP instead of just ahead.

Do you feel as if your spirit has been shattered? Have you been hurt, let down, or disappointed? Do you feel as if your circumstances are more than you can possibly endure? CHOOSE to change your mind and the way you see... focus on all the GOOD things, the GOOD people, everything that HAS gone your way! Find your "mojo" again and guard it now more than ever! Don't let anyone or any situation take it away!

Do not pay attention to the events of the past, the things that are old! New things are headed your way!!! A path will be made for you! Look ahead with a bright, new clear vision!!!

Investing in others' lives can help heal your pain.

You will experience your anxieties, thoughts, and situations just like the waves of a tossing sea: some moments are pleasant and some are torment. Learn to trust your inner peace to guide you through these times. Tell yourself to relax, take a deep breath, and focus on the positive (when you do this, what you should focus on comes to you). Believe it's all good even if it's bad, knowing it all works together like the pieces of a puzzle. You don't have to be thankful FOR it, just be thankful IN it. It WILL be okay... perhaps not today or tomorrow...But in time, dear....
I promise!

Live your great purpose! Live for what matters!

This year you may have been down paths, roads, valleys, rivers and streams you never ever thought you'd have to go down. You've had to make choices and deal with situations that you never thought imaginable. You've experienced pain that you never thought you could endure....But, sunshine, you did it! It may not have been easy and you certainly didn't see it coming your way BUT you've done it. You now have discovered a greater depth of life, a deeper appreciation which has made you a different person. Use all you have experienced (good and bad) to help others through their personal valleys, creating a domino effect of MGFL. There is no greater joy than helping fill the void, the hole in a hurting heart!

Don't miss the MESSAGE in the midst of your trials and storms!

Did you ever watch the old "I Dream of Jeanie" show? Remember when she would get locked in her bottle and she couldn't get out? She would bang from the inside and yell, "LET ME OUT!!!" Do you feel like that in your life? You aren't here to feel trapped! You are here for a specific purpose! Go about your day with simply that promise... Knowing you have a reason for being!!! You may or may not know that reason clearly at the moment...However, there's promise! You aren't going to miss your purpose! Dear, you aren't in charge of that! The opportunity for your purpose will make its own way! So smile today and put an extra skip in your step!

If the grass looks greener on the other side, try fertilizing your side!

When your spirit is broken for whatever reason, be courageous, dear, in your thoughts and efforts knowing that your heart WILL be filled again! That broken feeling may return now and again but you have the strength to keep your joy! Attack that feeling, keep that strength and power! Keep it front and center! Do not allow other PEOPLE or SITUATIONS to cast a shadow on your spirit! The way you are is just as you've been designed! Delight in that and let others see your delight, so they will delight in it too!!!

If your challenges can be fixed with the dollar bill then don't "freak out" too much about them, dear!

Do you feel as if you live life in a pressure cooker? Do you feel like you are about to EXPLODE? Take a deep breath, sunshine! It's time to reduce responsibilities and stop trying to do it all...Let go! Do what REALLY matters, things that will ultimately make a difference. Yes, laundry needs to be done, dinner needs to be made, etc... However, it's all the little, meaningless things we do in between that overwhelm us! Take a step back to look at your life, be vulnerable and perhaps ask others what they see you doing that you could eliminate (sometimes we can't see it ourselves). All of this is for your benefit, not for your detriment, sunshine. You and your stress levels are the thermostat in your home... Keep it a comfortable climate for everyone!

Keep moving forward, sunshine, even when you don't feel like it. Step by step, little by little it WILL get better!

Have you ever stood in front of a microwave while waiting for something to heat up and watched the time tick down? Have you ever wondered what just happened to change someone's life forever in those few seconds? Do you appreciate each second of your life? Those are seconds that will never be replaced, never changed, never undone. Keeping that time clock that constantly counts down in the front of your mind as you go through your day can help you to appreciate life. Appreciate each second the very best you can!

Unreasonable panic, disturbing unsettledness, struggling constantly with an uneasy feeling that won't go away??? You battle a heaviness, a torment in the pit of your stomach. It rides on your shoulders and weighs you down...You WILL emerge remarkable, refined and resilient due to this battle you have conquered day by day, moment by moment!

Control your thoughts or they will control you!

Stop living in the RAW! Does your heart seem like a piece of raw meat? Have you grown accustomed to hurt, pain, disappointment and the feeling of defeat? Stop dwelling on how RAW you feel and start looking at and living the joy! Start EXPECTING joy... It is there...Seek it!

You may feel lonely but you are NOT alone, my friend!

Are you smiling on the outside and crying on the inside? You look at everyone around you and their lives seem perfect. Not so, dear!! Everyone lacks in something!!! At some point everyone's heart aches about something. And sometimes when you hit bottom you find out what you are all about! Discover YOU!!!

BELIEVE that BETTER and BEST await you, dear!!!

Don't let the past dictate who you are! Don't let your past mistakes control your future! When you know better, you do better! Look FORWARD!

There are times when we gripe, whine and complain about our situations and circumstances. However, we just may be IN those because it's saving us from something worse! Perhaps that delay, that stall, that bump in the road saved us from making a huge mistake. Great things are revealed when you get to the point in life when your circumstances don't matter…you decide nothing can steal your joy!

Do not avoid making necessary changes in your life! Sometimes you have to go through the "yucky" to get to the "yummy!"

EASE the storm of your heart! It WILL work out; it always does, even though you cannot see it right now! Just trust, believe, have faith, keep stepping in a positive direction - one baby step at a time if that's what it takes! You will arrive at your destination!

If you aren't being YOU then a position on earth isn't being filled! You are unique, special and designed for a specific purpose! You are loved just the way are...Just Be You!

Don't doubt for one second that what you may think is impossible.... IS POSSIBLE!!! Trust, have faith, believe from deep within! ANYTHING CAN HAPPEN! That, my friend, is a promise!

Just seek your true purpose and your path will become clear!!!

Sometimes you are drained from every source so you will trust THE SOURCE!

Arriving at every mountain top requires that you climb through the valley. That's why when you reach the peak, the view and the feeling of victory are unmatchable! Keep climbing, sunshine, keep climbing!!!

Challenges create strength! Be Strong!

Adversity and affliction have expiration dates – they won't last forever. Stay strong and look for the wisdom during your storm. Though you think it's not fair, things aren't what you had hoped, you are disappointed and overwhelmed, you never know - these "road bumps" may have saved you from crashing completely!!! With that thought in mind, take a step outside your current point of view and look at your situation with new eyes. It will be okay...Just trust!!!

Your charm is the mirror of your heart!

Sunshine, sometimes you just have to do what's right for your heart! Even if it doesn't make sense to anyone else!

What you think about is what you get!

True wisdom knows every story has TWO sides!

Choose your words CAREFULLY - they can uplift or they can damage. Damage repair takes time. It's like hammering a nail into a wooden post and then pulling the nail out. The nail has been removed but the hole stays! Your words can be forgiven but the scar remains. Careful, dear!

Before accomplishment there must be desire! The desire must be strong, determined and confident!

An empty stomach can create a clear mind. Consider fasting (of course, check with your doctor first).

Where there is determination, a way, a path, a direction can be found! Determination can lead you out of difficulties and into the happiness and joy of success! Discover the power of determination!

Sometimes wisdom comes by way of wounds (unfortunately).

Action will guide you forward to the success you desire! Step out!

A candle loses none of its flame by giving light to another candle!

Don't see things as AWFUL see them as AWE-FULL!

Those who love you don't make fun of the stupid, silly things you do... They overlook them and see you for who you truly are!

Zig when others are zagging! Be different! Be creative! Be memorable! Stand out from the crowd and create a positive "buzz!"

Sometimes you simply just have to agree to disagree!

Don't become frustrated - stay the course! Sometimes the course is longer than you think but there is a finish line! You'll cross it if you stay focused and determined!

You aren't here to simply exist - you are here because you matter!!!

Be radiant, sunshine! Allow your heart to beat and your mind to fill with joy!

Use the difficulties and challenges you've faced to help others in a special way.

Changing the way you think can change your life!

Some situations in life are like eating junk food! It's exciting and tasty to take a bite, but the taste only lasts for a short time and the repercussions aren't worth it! So be careful not to get into the habit of junk!!! Not just food!

Perhaps you are in a place in your life right now that you NEED to be (though you might not WANT to be there!) to get closer to where you need to STAY!

If you don't spend time and energy on great ideas, they certainly won't become a reality!

You hold me up... I'll hold you up! That's what girlfriends do!

Let your light shine! No matter what you are going through keep your inner flame lit! You will be guided if you keep your heart open! Don't become cold and hard, sunshine...Yes, it's SO hard when you have either had someone wrong you or you know you've done something wrong, but decide to grow from the good and the bad. Here is a promise...Your light WILL end up shining through the darkness!

You are truly rich when you can love someone you used to hate.

Enjoy every moment!

Sticks and stones may break your bones...but words CAN hurt you! Words can hurt way more than any physical injury! Fortunately, words are POWERUL healers, as well: they can uplift, motivate, speak volumes, heal hearts and encourage!!!

There IS a difference between forgiving and forgetting (remember, though, forgiving releases you).

Whatever your race, gender, social position, political views, job, financial situation, etc...You will not be judged - Not here!!! You are SPECIAL, you are LOVED, you have PURPOSE...YOU BELONG!!!

It's time for a period of pleasant moments. Start thinking of ways to 'improve' and 'remove' in your life to make a difference.

One day the movie of your life may flash before your eyes... Make sure it's a movie worth watching!

Sometimes we are tested in the "furnace of affliction." Remember, sunshine...This refines us, develops us, allows us to grow, helps us endure and gain inner strength. If we don't allow growth from within, we will never know what we are capable of accomplishing!

Sometimes in chasing perfection, your own imperfections show up.

If you believe in something...fight for it!

Don't let anyone or anything take away your joyful spirit! Just be you!

Be VERY, VERY careful in forming your opinions...
You may think you know the details, but do you really???
Everyone has their opinions and they are completely
entitled to them... However, there are always many angles
to a situation...You do not know what others have been
through or are going through....be VERY careful, dear,
before forming your opinion!!!

Anger is one letter off from Danger. It's a powerful,
destructive emotion... Handle your anger carefully. Give
yourself time to consider your anger before reacting or
the results could be devastating. However, anger can be
used as fuel to help you get out of a situation you would
have otherwise tolerated. Either way, be very careful
with this emotion.

Do you know what you want? What is it???

When you feel as if you are being criticized, judged, or condemned by others...Stand tall knowing you have done your best! If you have made a mistake, ask for forgiveness and remember that everyone makes mistakes. If feel you haven't done anything wrong, remain firm in your position without being offensive. It can be hard to feel judged...Those doing the judging think they see the whole picture, but it's really like a puzzle still being put together... The picture looks one way but there are still pieces missing. The picture of your situation would change entirely for those forming their opinion of you if they had those pieces. Try not to take their opinion too much to heart.

People you love will unfortunately disappoint you and let you down... Remember, they are only human... We all make mistakes... Give people ROOM to make mistakes, to correct them and to grow from them... We will all be better and closer as a result!

When you are battered, bruised, beaten by the events of life...Remember you DO have the strength to endure! We MUST endure, we CAN endure... we have no choice! It's a moment by moment battle! We all have different battles to fight, but know there is "MGFL" here for you!!!

You matter – Period!

My dear, you are not alone, you are loved, you are provided with inner strength, you are provided with all the tools you need...Sometimes you just need a little reminder, a little nudge to push you! Keep moving forward, sunshine! It WILL be alright! Be strong! Be YOU!

Allow your inner being to be empowered and strengthened so you can complete the purpose for which you were designed. My dear, you DO have great purpose!

RELAX, dear. You will NOT miss the opportunity for your purpose to be fulfilled. Sunshine, you aren't THAT powerful....Someone else is, though!

When your heart is raw, your soul is weak, your mind is overloaded and your body is exhausted, keep your mind focused on what is good, true, pure, lovely, right and just! Do not despair, dear. Stay on the path and it will lead you to peace and contentment that even the wealthiest of wealthy cannot buy!

There are so many people who live in mental bondage, mental jail, beating themselves up inside over and over for things that should have been, things that could have been, things they wish they could go back and change. Don't live there, sunshine! You have the key to unlock your jail cell! Unlock it, come out and don't go back! Catch yourself before you begin to be trapped in that mental bondage. That's not how your life should be lived. Make peace and move forward! Yes, it's easier said than done... One baby step at a time is how you get there!

Forgiving is like a "get out of jail free" card –It is your ticket to release you from the bondage of holding a grudge. Set YOURSELF free.

You've gotta call a spade a spade… It is what it is!

Sometimes you just have to look in the mirror and say, "Babe, you've done the best you know how…I'm proud of you!"

If you try to fix and control everything, you are going to wear yourself out! Trust and surrender, dear!

We WANT to be made of iron and steel, however we ARE made of flesh and blood...It's okay to feel a little vulnerable sometimes.

Be careful of consuming "junk food!" – Not just eating foods without nutritional value, but what you think about, what you talk about, what actions you take, what you watch on TV, etc... Things that are NO GOOD for you! Feast on what truly "feeds" you for your own good! Fuel your mind, body and spirit to be healthy in every area!

Don't let circumstances dictate the degree of your happiness, your joy, and your outlook!

That which doesn't kill us makes us stronger!

When you have conquered a vice, a temptation, a habit, or a destructive situation even just ONE time you are moving in the right direction! It takes baby steps sometimes to overcome and to renew yourself. One victory at a time will lead you to your ultimate goal!

Correct/positive/successful living comes from correct/positive/successful thinking!

YES! You MUST have girl time regardless of your age or stage in life... PERIOD!

Even though we love her, Barbie is over 50, made of plastic, isn't married and doesn't have children or a job...ummmm... EXACTLY! We've been set up since childhood with unrealistic expectations! No fair! It's funny that we love Barbie because she has everything and we don't like Barbie because she has everything!

Buying a new pair of shoes is like taking a good dose of medicine - It always works!

Do not live in gloom and despair... That is NOT how we are to live life! Look around you right this minute and notice three simple things that are amazing in your life! Guaranteed you'll find way more than three! Not living in gloom and despair starts with keeping your mind right! Sometimes that's not just a daily challenge but a moment-by-moment challenge! Build upon one "fabbbulows" thought at a time to increase your joy! (Read the story behind "fabbbulows" on www.thegirlfriendbook.com)

You were designed and placed here to make a difference. When you fully understand and grasp that concept, your life, your vision, your day-to-day steps will completely change!

Be careful with what you complain about, sunshine...
There are plenty of people out there who would give
anything to be YOU!

What if this is as good as it gets?! Are you making the
most of it?

When metal is purified, it's heated until the impurities
rise to the top. This part is skimmed off, leaving nothing
but the BEST for further usage. Skim off the unnecessary
items within your life leaving only the "good parts" that will
be of benefit. Life is too precious to focus on the impurities.
Choose to focus on what's good, right, motivating,
encouraging and positive!!!

Be like a cat - always land on your feet!

Where did you leave the old you??? Go get her and tell her to come out and play! Put on some happy music then dance around your living room. WHO CARES who's watching? Perhaps they will even join you! OH, GO AHEAD!!!

Love is more priceless and lasting than any other gift: it cannot be purchased because it is freely given and received. It cannot be destroyed by the hour glass or by natural disaster. Real love is a true gift! Be thankful for it, treasure it and take good care of it!

Seek & Find

Darling, you are BEAUTIFUL!

To obtain balance in your life you need self-control. Self- control is achieved only by relying on the strength within. I promise that if you search for that strength it WILL be given to you.

I can promise you that these two things done constantly will change your life: DAILY QUIET TIMES and EXCERCISE. Make yourself do them!!!

The answer to a dilemma often lies in the conviction you feel within. Act upon that burning placed in the center of your chest! Listening to your inner voice will never lead you in the wrong direction! When in doubt, follow it, sunshine!

You can't wait around for things or situations to just fall into your lap. Get up, get out and make something happen! That is called...FAITH!

Don't allow your mistakes to consume you! Decide to learn from them and do not repeat them. Everyone messes up! Forgive yourself and move in a healthy direction!

Life is too short not to think BIG!

Don't give up! Keep going! Stay positive! Refuse to surrender! You WILL see the results of your efforts!

Time has a way of making our memories "fuzzy." Remember to journal in detail about events and the way you felt. Retaining the raw emotions will help you when you read back over it by guiding you toward seeing that each experience in life (good and bad) has a purpose.

When talking to someone, LISTEN to them and try to avoid turning the story to being about you. Ask them questions, focus on them. We often take over a conversation before we realize what we've done! Be concerned and interested... Let them talk about themselves...There are times when people solve their own problems by simply "talking" it out. By truly listening, you might be helping someone more than you can imagine.

If you have fallen short of.... Whatever...That's OKAY! Just decide it's time to rebuild, refocus, regroup and move on!! BooYah!

PASSION is the secret ingredient, the fill-in-the-blank, the missing puzzle piece, the difference maker!!! Find your passion and act on it and change your life.

Why is it in commercials you see the mom baking in a SUPER clean kitchen, using perfectly pre-portioned ingredients, divided into cute little bowls? She is perfectly dressed up, smiling like everything is right with life and then...sweet, cute, clean little kids come skipping in to snatch a perfectly round, non-burnt cookie... Whose world is like that?!?! RRRRIGGGHT!!! Have a good REAL day, sunshine!!!

EXPECT good, positive, happy things to happen for you!!! They WILL!!!

If you are going south on the highway and you realize you need to be going north, at some point you MUST turn around! You must change directions! You cannot keep doing the same thing and expect a different result!

You may have a big dream but not a clue how it can be accomplished. If that dream is burning within, KEEP GOING, dear, because if you do, your talents, efforts, influences and resources will supernaturally multiply! Do not give up! You have been given this dream and this desire for a purpose!

Be Strong! Be You!

You CAN enjoy your life if you so choose! Choose to take action on purpose to live peacefully, happily and joyfully!!!

Sometimes it takes just as much energy to avoid a task as to go ahead and do it! Don't procrastinate - get it off your to do list!

Value every person you meet. You take a little bit of each person you encounter along with you in your life. You never know what simple thing someone did or said that may be passed along through you to better your life or someone else's!

A changed mind is a changed direction!

There are things you have done, mistakes you have made that you would do anything to erase! But, from those circumstances you now will do anything you can not to repeat them again, to stay away from and out of the "hole" you dug for yourself in the past. This makes you BETTER, sunshine! It's all good!

You will be restored, sunshine... Believe, trust and have faith! Those are the simple ingredients to success! (Note that having faith means taking action upon your beliefs.) Do not give negative thoughts "miracle grow"... STOP feeding them by dwelling on them and they will stop growing like weeds! Intentionally stop thinking about them and immediately start thinking about something positive! It's amazing how this simple task can change your life!

Sometimes the lessons we learn are painful but the experiences are necessary for us to learn. Use the pain as "fuel for your fire" to make you better!

Be okay with your "imperfections." NO ONE is perfect, sunshine! Being okay with your imperfections makes you GORGEOUS, Dahhhling!!!

Learn to reduce (or at least manage) your stress - it's just a part of life! Develop a relationship with it 'cause it's not going anywhere!

Go about your day asking yourself, "How many lives can I touch today in a positive way?" This will not only enhance, impact and encourage others, but it will do the same for your own life as well! We have enough in this world going on that brings us down - let's lift each other up!

You can work yourself too hard and become anxious trying to "make it all happen;" you may lose sleep worrying; wear yourself out trying to obtain many material possessions. Don't go around chasing the wind...Leave your legacy through providing wisdom, knowledge, guidance and happiness to others!!!

When others let you down and disappoint you...There IS someone who won't, never will and never has!

MGFL!

When you feel empty inside, like you have a bleeding heart, internally raw, as if you have a hole in your chest... Take one moment at a time, one day at a time; pray; think and say positive things to yourself; exercise; focus on everything that is good in your life. Believe!!!

When you need to have a confrontation with someone, just go ahead and get it over with. It's better to just deal with it than to let it eat you up inside.

There are times you just have to "ride the wave." Hold tight...it WON'T last forever. And it certainly makes you appreciate the still waters when you've endured the "white caps" of life.

If you are spinning around trying to figure everything out, you will spend a lifetime doing it. Simply surrender it, dear. It will all be taken care of!

Are you in a dark, unhappy, lonely, low place? You don't want to be there, but what can you do??? Start by putting on new eyes. TRY to look at things from a different perspective (after all, the way you are looking at it now is getting you...where?!?). Try hard to capture things in a different way - Like putting on a new pair of prescription glasses! Once you see more CLEARLY your heart will start to feel differently. It's a start!

Even though we get frustrated with the delays in our lives, sometimes the delays themselves are our answer.

When you are dealing with a challenge that you are trying to conquer, write it all out on a piece of paper and then crumple it up and throw it in the trash can. This gesture to yourself symbolizes that you are ridding yourself of the burden of that challenge.

It takes great self- control to be addressed harshly and not to respond in kind. A soft answer to harsh treatment will defuse the situation and avoid further argument.

We do not need to constantly defend ourselves to others. You know where you stand. Be okay with that and stop feeling like you have to explain yourself to people all the time.

Wise people know how and when to remain silent but foolish people sometimes blurt out their thoughts.

Pressures and influences of society can steer us in the wrong direction before we even realize what happened. If you find you've "fallen off the horse" in your life, just get right back on and keep riding.

Peace comes from above...Period.

When situations get "sticky," the first thing most of us feel like doing is escaping - running away from the problem. That really isn't the best solution. Hold tight…you may not be able to get OUT of dealing with the problem, but strength will be provided for you to get THROUGH it! You WILL make it through!

You can't put a price tag on the feeling of peace.

Are you looking up at the climb ahead of you and asking yourself, "DANG… how steep is this staircase???" Just take it one step at a time!

Celebrate YOU today! Go do something nice for yourself!

When one door closes another one opens. Unfortunately, sometimes we have to hang out in the hallway for awhile until the right door opens! Hang tight!!

Take time to really examine your projects, your goals, what you choose to spend your time and efforts on. What is your starting point, your foundation, your motivation for each one of these? Is it meaningful and purposeful?

We can chase the wind, but we can't hold or keep it. The same is true of our accomplishments if they come and go leaving us with a feeling of temporary happiness. Feel the wind on your face, however, as you pursue things that are fulfilling, meaningful, purposeful, and have solid foundations. You can't take people or things with you when you go but you have a purpose (whether small, medium or large) that will leave an imprint on the world after you are gone.

When you are trying hard to let go of a difficult situation within your heart, it's helpful to have a mental visual of letting it go, releasing it, and freeing yourself. Go to the grocery store and get one of the free balloons they give away, write on the balloon with a marker the situation, issue, hurt, or challenge you are dealing with, take it outside, look up and LET GO!!!

To conquer insecurities and low self-esteem you must change how you think of yourself on an emotional level. Start telling yourself, "You ARE good enough! You ARE worthy!" Perhaps your idea of what you "should be" really isn't realistic. Stop judging yourself and comparing yourself to others. The standards of today are CRAZY!!! If you could really see others behind closed doors you would learn that NO ONE is perfect, sunshine! It's time to love yourself!!!

Be cautious, careful and aware of your influences, the company you keep, and the decisions you make because you become a slave to whatever masters you. Don't let those things entangle you and don't let anyone control you like a puppet! Stand up for what you believe in, what is right, what is honorable, and what works for you and your family. If you don't stand for something, you'll fall for anything. Be on guard and stay secure in your position.

To "preach" means to "make known," so consider yourself a preacher and preach what you know to who you know! Let's learn from each other's experiences and life lessons. It's a sick feeling not to be able to afford your life. Adjust your lifestyle to be more comfortable. That nauseous feeling isn't worth anything extra you might want to buy. Before you purchase something think about when the bill comes due... After the thrill is gone and it's time to pay up will it ultimately be worth it?!?! You had better love that purchase more than the feeling of the money in your pocket.

Sunshine, remain clear-minded and self- controlled. This world has us so busy we can feel like hamsters running around on a wheel. It's hard to see things clearly. Step off that wheel, let yourself slow down and make sure you are seeing things for what they really are.

You can lose material possessions, but you can't lose wisdom, knowledge and character. Choose to spend time on issues that REALLY matter.

Just as iron shapes iron, we are here to help shape, guide and mold each other for great purposes. Share with someone else all you have been through. You will either find that they needed your guidance or that they have been through their fair share of being molded and shaped and perhaps you can learn from them.

Abundance isn't always about material gains. It can be about wisdom and knowledge! Wisdom and knowledge come from experience...sometimes from the TOUGHEST experiences. Gaining abundance in that respect is truly priceless.

Telling the truth to someone who asks your opinion is like hooking them up to an IV. The needle hurts at first; however, the medicine gets to the blood stream quickly and relieves the pain faster... The same goes for telling people the truth!

When you feel desperate for answers, you must be very careful where you look for those answers.

Integrity battles are won or lost in the heart.

Don't live your life feeling trapped! Your life has meaning and purpose! What has happened has happened... Don't let the past keep you from deciding that it's time to move forward!

Choose happiness - it's free!

As you improve your life others will naturally be drawn to you. When they are, you can share with them how you grew and how they can achieve a fulfilled life as well. When you give to others in this way, you feed your heart and soul!

Use visual reminders such as quotes, verses, sayings or pictures to help keep you on track. Post them on your bathroom mirror, on your refrigerator, in your car, etc... to help you stay focused on being a better you mentally, physically and emotionally!

You say you "aren't taking any applications" for new friends? What if some of the greatest friends you will ever have haven't met you yet? Understand that being more selective as you get older doesn't mean you need to become closed-minded.

In ALL circumstances, find joy! Yes, ALL circumstances! Sometimes it's hard and you can't see any reason to be joyful... SEARCH for those reasons, love, and they will be there.

Feel like a ticking time bomb? Feel like you are walking on a tightrope? You can't keep up an insane pace or you will either explode or come crashing down!!! Something has to give! Remember your priorities and adjust accordingly! You don't have to be intelligent to be smart!

You have control over most of your choices, so exercise that control and choose wisely.

There is a point where you aren't effective because you are trying too hard. Sometimes you have to slow down instead and relax a little to be effective.

Live in assurance, sunshine!

If you try to control, chisel and mold those around you, they will run from your efforts. Resign from the job of trying to "fix" everyone and everything. Work on fixing YOURSELF and simply love everyone else.

Free yourself of the slavery of trying to be perfect! No one has everything!

The longer you stay in a situation the more it becomes commonplace to you and your excitement leaves. If you feel you are on a mission, heading down a path of purpose in your situation, try to remember how you felt at the beginning of that path and recapture that feeling! Keep the flutter in your heart alive!

You can control what you say, what you think, whether or not you keep your temper, etc... You don't need to be anxious, worried or upset. Give it all over - it will all be okay if you will simply trust and obey. Don't let anything steal your joy!

Self- destruction, addictions, bad habits...Recognize and admit your weaknesses as the first steps to correction. Then reach out and help someone who has the same challenge!

Sometimes we run from the very tools that are being used to shape and mature us. Begin to recognize these tools and allow them to work on you so that you can grow!

Be secure in who YOU ARE so you don't allow people around you to wound you!

Be strong and confident in your abilities so you don't need to have people tell you how great you are all the time.

As you age, learn to guard what you say. Have you ever noticed that older people are less likely to babble than younger people? With age comes wisdom.

It's miserable to be uneasy. This is often because you are doing something you shouldn't be doing but you don't want to give it up. You'd rather ignore it than deal with it. At some point you must decide to deal with it and make it right.

Get a grip! Stop saying, "If only I had this or that I would be happy." There will always be something more you want.   You need to learn to be happy no matter what.

Refuse to sit around and think about how bad everything is for you...Stop that negative thought process before it brings you down. If you can keep it from getting into your mind, it won't get into your heart. Protect your heart and mind, sunshine!

To get the negative out of your life SPEAK the positive.

If one of your problems is worrying about who has "more" than you, then you need to GIVE! Do the opposite of your problem and you will solve it!

Simply put, be strong!

"A true answer is like a kiss on the lips!" Did you know that a long time ago a kiss on the lips was a sign of true friendship? Show your true friendship: When asked your opinion, tell the truth... Just say it nicely.

Being comfortable with your imperfections makes you more attractive! No one is perfect. People won't notice your "imperfections" (or what you may think are imperfections) when you are at ease with them and not drawing attention to them.

It's amazing how everything is always someone else's fault! Nope... Not always! Let's stop playing 'the blame game' and simply move forward with what we need to deal with. Dwelling on who did what doesn't really get us any further ahead.

I think I can...I think I can...I think I can...Choo Choo!! Mistakes don't have to be failures. Failures happen only when you don't learn your lesson.

Sometimes you think you need a word of encouragement when, in fact, you need a word of correction! Ouch!

Patience is knowing it will happen and allowing the time for it to happen!

Stop running from reality. Face it knowing you have the ability to hold strong, to learn and to grow!

Failure doesn't have to be final. Failure has the potential to be the launching pad for the next great phase of our lives.

Not every bad thing is a truly bad thing... Look for blessings in EVERYTHING.

Money only makes some of your problems go away.... Focus on resolving the internal ones through personal growth!

Apply what you have learned in your heart. Grow from the wisdom you have obtained.

Sometimes you are so broken that the only thing that will fix your spirit is to give of yourself to others. Give and your spirit will be mended!

What if wives and husbands treated each other the same way throughout the years as they did the day they got married???

Dream while you are awake!

Sometimes things don't get easier, they just get less hard.

Money makes life more convenient - not more fulfilling!

Desire is much like salty ocean water - the more you drink the thirstier you become!

One of the biggest reasons people do not get what they want is because of fear. Tackle your fears to overcome your obstacles. It will be a new world for you, sunshine! Fear is a great way to hold yourself back. Don't allow it! Push through and conquer your fears!!!

It's incredible the lengths you will go to (sometimes good, sometimes not so good) for something or someone you hold dear.

When you clean out your refrigerator the best way to clean it well is to remove everything and then scrub it. Think of your mind in the same way... Sometimes you need to clear it out of all the thoughts and worries and get away from distractions in order to get it really clean!

Some days are like diamonds that shine when the light hits them just right. Other days are like dust that looks dull and yucky no matter how the light hits it. Hope you have a diamond day, sunshine!

Your children and grandchildren need to hear, see and feel the strength and security you have within you! It's time to STOP the generational curse of insecurity! Set strong, confident examples!

There are many things we can't comprehend...why/
how/it's not fair/why me? Even though these aspects
are unclear to us now... rest assured, dear, you WILL
be alright! It's so hard not to be anxious, not to worry
and not to have a heavy heart, but your concerns will be
taken care of! That's a promise! You will look
back one day and see it much more clearly!

If you feel you have no joy in your life, then, sweetie, you
are looking for joy in the wrong places!

Perhaps it's time to move on, to move forward...

Whenever appropriate, may your touch be gentle and your words soft.

You don't need to search out people to tell you how great and wonderful you are. You ARE great and wonderful! Just LIVE it! Know who you are!

Be secure, strong and stable! You don't need validation from other people! Believe in yourself and then you will be open to the plan for your life. You'll never please everyone so don't waste your time trying! Stop it!

Go spend time on who and what really matter!

Push and follow through, dear, push and follow through!

Guard your mind! Remember garbage in, garbage out!

Expect God to move in your life all the time. Seek him and the rest will be taken care of.

Don't let anyone or anything steal your joy!!!

When you are enjoying what you are doing, when you are smiling, project your joy - it changes everything!

Keep your light shining from within! It's hard to keep it lit when the wind is blowing, but keep the flame protected! Fire is an essential element of life. Guard it with all your might, for you are super-special!

A happy heart creates a cheerful face. A happy heart is good medicine for all who come in contact with you! You have no idea what your smile might do for someone else today!

When you start justifying things, then something's up!
Be aware, sunshine!

If you feel pressured to make a decision on the spot that
you are uncomfortable with, LISTEN to your inner
voice! Wait for the right decision. When it comes along,
you'll know because it will all work out smoothly. Allow
the peace of your heart to rule!

There are moments when it seems as if there is no way
through an impossible situation, but there is, my dear,
there is! Stay strong, stay focused and believe that you
can overcome any obstacle. It won't be like this forever!

Sometimes all it takes is one person to believe in you to help you accomplish what you thought you couldn't!

It's okay to enjoy a little personal satisfaction in proving someone wrong who said you couldn't do it!

If you are feeling down, write down all your blessings.

Discernment = A wise heart!

How we react to our problems determines how long we will stay in them. The way to handle problems is to go straight through them and DEAL with them. Don't try to go around them or over them – just go directly through the middle and HANDLE them!

Sometimes things can be "said" with total silence.

Real abundance is not what you own - it's who you are and what you stand for within yourself.

Sometimes the best way to HEAR is to sit in silence.

If you can't rejoice right now, then you aren't focused on the right things. Understand that if you rejoice, everything else will take care of itself!

Unfortunately, sometimes we have to fail in order to succeed.

You will find that success comes more easily when you are in proper alignment with your purpose!

We go through pain and suffering partly so that we can be used as tools for encouraging, motivating, and supporting others. Don't let your pain and suffering go without purpose! Reach out to others who can relate to you, learn from you and grow from within because of your experiences! We need each other!

Some people use invisible fencing to keep their beloved pets from wandering off or running out into danger. The pet wears a collar that 'buzzes' them if they get close to the 'fence' that protects them, warning them to stay inside the fence and away from danger. Similarly, sometimes things happen in our lives that make our 'collar' go off and BUZZ us! Remember, love, it's for our protection, for our own good, to knock us back in line and keep us from danger!

Give purposeful thought to every step you take!
Extend and embrace love and receive divine friendship!

Control the words that come out of your mouth. If
you're not careful, they can be like knives stabbed directly
into the heart. Once the harm has been done, you can
never undo it. Words are powerful weapons; make sure
you are well trained before you wield them!

All people are motivated by their needs and discouraged
by their fears. We are together in the uphill battle to succeed.
Together we will!

Be inspired and Be inspiring!
Be excited and Be exciting!
Be interested and Be interesting!

Today is a new day, sunshine! So give yourself a new beginning...Start over by creating a new foundation for yourself! YES, you CAN do this!

Never forget who you are!

KNOWING the needs of others and MEETING those needs are completely different things. Follow through!

If you want to have friends, be FRIENDLY!

If you will give of yourself, you will prosper.

There is an opportunity to see things differently if you will simply allow yourself to do so!

Stop working on your PhD in Problems; get a Masters in Solutions instead. Go make something happen!

This world seems to condition us for the worst. Instead, EXPECT the BEST!

Meet adversity with a smile! Stay positive!

Hard times produce deep souls!!!

Keep your priorities balanced: #1 Spiritual Life, #2 Family, #3 Friends, #4 Work.

We live in a "disposable" world, but don't treat people like fast food containers! Love on people; give them your time and energy! It will be returned to you!

If you wait to be happy until everyone likes you, you will never be happy. YOU need to like YOURSELF, sunshine! You ARE SPECIAL!

You are a beautiful light! Shine! Don't let anyone blow your light out!

Don't worry about things that are temporary!

Do you want financial security? Give away 10% of what you make FIRST, pay yourself 10% next, then live off the rest. Adjust your lifestyle accordingly.

There will ALWAYS be housework! Take time to enjoy your friends, family, children... Enjoy your time!

How much money would it take to make you happy? No matter how much you have, the answer will always be more than what you have. Learn to receive contentment!

The only person who fails is the one who quits! Don't quit!

Be careful as you rise to success that it doesn't draw you away from what is most important. Don't lose focus on WHO you are and WHAT you are here to do!

There is no pain like parental pain! Yes, there will be disappointments and hurts but you must keep directing, leading and loving them unconditionally! The joy they bring as a result will be unmatched! They are given to you as the most precious gifts - treasure and nurture those gifts!

Be careful not to get so preoccupied with the mechanics of life that you forget what REALLY matters in life!

Marriage is not a fantasy - Needs and wants change as you get older. The timeline looks something like this:

Years 1 - 2: Young love (probably no children)

Years 3 - 10: Realistic love

Years 11 - 25: Comfortable love

Years 26 - 35: Renewing love

Years 36 - over: Transcendent love

Watch what you read, what you look at, and the company you keep. You become just what you expose yourself to!

Arrogant pride leads to disgrace, which leads to humility, which leads to WISDOM! Stay humble, dear, and get to the 'wisdom' part sooner!

Ronald Reagan said: "Trust, but verify."

This is great advice because we need to believe in people or we won't have relationships. In business and personal situations, we must put our trust in others but at the same time, we must protect ourselves. This is a great thought to have in mind if you find yourself vulnerable in situations.

Remember to KISS your life: Keep It Simple, Silly!!! Simple is better!

Life is hard...Period. Just never forget that you aren't alone, sunshine!

Go forward each day growing in knowledge and grace! Leave a legacy for future generations that shows them you were here fulfilling your purpose. Your purpose can be to raise your family, touch the lives of others, grow a company of great influence, etc... No purpose is too big or too small!

When your feet can't hold you up any longer, your knees will!

Think of all you are going through as stepping stones of life, leading you on your path of purpose. Remember, love, now is not forever.

You may not be where you WANT to be right now, but you may be where you NEED to be for now. HERE, you can grow as a person and make adjustments to your life you normally wouldn't attempt. Try your best to look at where you are right now with new eyes.

Listen to your inner voice - it's your inner "navigation system," so let it guide you on your path. It's never wrong! Sometimes we can't hear it because it gets drowned out by our busy-ness or we ignore its pull. Make an effort to listen for it and to follow it…Pay attention, sunshine, and it will lead you on your path.

You listen to someone and think, "Why are they complaining? Look how good they have it?!?!" Sweetie, someone is looking at you the very same way! Ummm?!?!

OUCH... Sometimes change is painful but necessary. Sometimes we feel raw, vulnerable, and helpless during change. Hang on tight, though, and you will make it through!

Smile even on the days you don't feel like it - it's hard but it helps!

At some point, everyone's bill comes due. Be careful, sunshine... and be sure you can pay for what you're choosing to buy – literally and otherwise!

Sunshine, control your thoughts or they will control YOU! Guard and guide your thought processes. This is a war zone; however, you can win the fight if you are aware of the battle! WIN, love, WIN!!!

You'll never make enough money to be rich if you don't know the value of what REALLY matters!!!

When making anything, PASSION should be your main ingredient!

You can't keep walking around carrying a backpack full of "rocks" (the burdens that weigh you down). One at a time, start removing the "rocks!" Life isn't meant to carry burdens... it's meant to spread JOY! And you can't SPREAD joy if you don't HAVE joy! Time for a change! Start by lightening your load! It may take time but you MUST do it!

When things are not going well, don't live in the worst case scenario. So many of us think of "how bad it will be" and live in it before it ever happens - and it usually never happens anyway! Don't make it worse before it is! That's a sure way to live unhappily unnecessarily.

A true friend accepts your past mistakes, encourages your future potential, and loves you just as you are.

Allow people time to get where they need to be...You can't force it. They need time to process, to realize, to deal with, to digest certain situations. Give that time to them, be there for them, patiently and unconditionally waiting with love!

You have no idea how much strength to endure you possess until you are forced to use it!

Sweetie, sometimes ya gotta do what ya gotta do! Do not worry about what people will think! They don't walk in your shoes...they don't know what you are going through.... So they don't have any right to judge! You must do what you believe is in your best interest.

Learn to make choices by looking long term. Perhaps delayed gratification would be a better decision. Don't be swayed by flashy "got to have it now" schemes. Think of how your choices will affect you now and later. Think through things using a long range thought process.

Wisdom isn't just knowledge; it is an ATTITUDE that affects every aspect of life.

The name of the game is "Keeping Calm and Carrying On!" It WILL all be okay.

'Confident' and 'Unstoppable' are two fabulous words!

What good are you to others? Seriously, dear... If you are going through hard times, make up your mind to use the experience of how you are getting through it with someone who needs guidance. You help them and YOURSELF by doing this. If you aren't going through difficulties or challenges at the moment, help someone in need with your time, money, love, etc... WHAT GOOD ARE YOU DOING? Whether large or small, you have a purpose to fulfill until the day you die!

Everyone deals with situations differently; allow others room to do what they need to do to get through - even if it's not what you would do or the way you would do it.

To help stop hurting inside, stop dwelling on your hurt. Sure, it's hard to do but try not to let your mind wander there. It's for your own "heart health!"

True grace and dignity mean saying you are sorry when you are wrong. We all mess up and make bad judgment calls sometimes but we don't need to punish ourselves forever. That doesn't do anyone any good! You miss out on lovely times and lovely people – and they miss out on lovely YOU! Life is too short... Just be sincere, ask for forgiveness, and forgive yourself.

Make sure the people in your life who are your "quiet force" (the people who are pulling for you behind the scenes no matter what) know that they are appreciated and how much they mean to you!

There are days you want to crawl in a hole or stay in bed with the sheets pulled over your head. You HAVE to pull yourself up and out! You can do it, sunshine! Remember, "They can take everything but they can't eat ya!"

Don't be a constant dripping faucet... Don't always be 'down' and looking for others to cheer you up. Those around you may love you dearly, however there is only so much they can take. When you always bring a black cloud with you they will simply start to stay away from you. It's okay to lean on your family and friends when you are in need - just be careful that you aren't ALWAYS in need.

If you keep going to someone with a problem (and you keep going over and over) and they give you advice...At some point, dear, you need to LISTEN and implement the advice or STOP asking them for it!!! They will eventually begin to think, "We must not really be friends because you aren't trusting me and listening to what I am trying to tell you!"

Give thanks through it all. There may be days when your world is crumbling, you are on the verge of giving up, you feel completely defeated, things are wrong and they only continue to get worse. All you can do is to get down on your knees. Unfortunately, sometimes it takes sinking to the bottom to get you there, but you WILL find what you need there on your knees! And it's the ONLY thing that will fill the hole in your soul.

There are times you just need to move forward (from people, careers, situations, experiences that have been hurtful or disappointing, etc.). Perhaps NOW is the time to 'cut your losses' and gain a fresh clean start.

Don't let petty things dominate your day or your thoughts. 'Sweating the small stuff' can control our thinking and, therefore, our actions. Before you know it, you'll find you've ended up busying yourself with doing a lot of petty things. You can't be productive, happy AND petty at the same time!

Try your best not to get worked up, grumpy or edgy when details need to be handled. Life will never be perfect, so you just need to learn to be flexible, love!

Do not doubt... If there is a pull on your heart and you have a dream, whatever it is CAN happen! Keep stepping out in faith and believing! Don't stop moving forward! Some days you may feel weak, but if there is a fire burning within your heart, you can find the strength to press ahead.

Write uplifting, positive sayings on post-it notes or postcards and put them in places you will see frequently – on the refrigerator, in your car or on your bathroom mirror - to constantly remind you to focus on positive thoughts.

When you are in the midst of difficult times, say to yourself, "I have the strength and power to endure; I have the strength and power to endure!" Yes you do, dear, yes you do!

When you are down, put on music, go read funny greeting cards, put your favorite movie on, go workout, buy a new pair of shoes, give yourself a facial mask, take a bite of chocolate or light some candles and enjoy a bubble bath Pamper yourself a bit, dear!

Don't beat yourself up... Remember you had to do what you had to do because you had no choice!

Have you been at "The Party" too long (the Pity Party, that is!!)? Worn out your welcome? Indulged yourself enough? Well, it's time to leave! The party's over, sunshine! Come on... Get up, get out, and get going, dear!!!

Sometimes you keep busy to avoid having to deal with "issues." The busier you are the less time you have to dwell on challenges. Sometimes that's helpful and sometimes it's not. Just be aware and dissect your issues carefully. Don't ignore problems that really need to be dealt with. But if there is nothing you can do about your situation, staying busy can be very helpful to your hurting heart! Don't fill your time with unnecessary "busy-ness." Don't confuse activity with productivity.

Don't let people lean on you so much that it knocks you over! You want to be there for others but not if it depletes YOU of strength!

The mad cycle of stress must be stopped! Remove stress from your life, sunshine... It's just not worth it!

Being kind to someone communicates to them that they matter, that they have value, and that they are important. Being kind is easy to do, so do it often.

Sometimes you need to just ZIP your LIP, sunshine! Control what you say! THINK before you SPEAK!

It's hard to stop trying to make everything and everyone "alright" all the time. If you don't stop, though, trying to keep it up will eventually lead you to implode! Take baby steps to begin to let go.

Make TODAY the day when you draw a line in the sand and say, "That's it... I'm starting new!"

Don't forget to look up and wink every once in awhile!

How you FEEL is directly related to what you THINK! Control your thoughts, sunshine!

Maybe you need to stop wasting time on the WHY of what's happened and figure out the HOW to move forward!

When you KNOW that you KNOW you should pursue something, don't put a question mark where a period has been placed! You gotta go where your heart is pulling you! GO FOR IT, BABE!!!

Selfless love is putting someone else first unconditionally.

Many of us desire "validation" from others. When you go through life always trying to please everyone, make everyone happy, and make everything perfect, the one person who is always "let down" is YOU! It is impossible to make everyone happy all the time. RELAX, love.

Try to deal with the issues at hand with a sincere heart. Powerful results are produced through true devotion.

Sometimes suffering shapes us - Darn it!!!

One of the greatest things you can do for yourself is to be STILL!

Sometimes you block yourself from 'feeling your feelings' because you let your past rule you. Try to release those past experiences and view life through a new set of eyes. It's AMAZING what you see when you are really looking! Unfortunately, sometimes all we have must be taken away in order for us to see everything we have that can never be taken away.

Stop focusing on what others have that you don't! You may have something they wish they could have (and I'm not only talking about material possessions). Their situation isn't better - it's just different. And the grass isn't greener on the other side - it's simply a different SHADE of green!

When did what you have become not good enough for you? What you have now was at one time, what you couldn't wait to get! Be CAREFUL with your thoughts, love! Be GRATEFUL for what you have right now.

Be your best at your profession, no matter what it is! It only takes trying just a little more than the next person, to stand out! If you are going to work, then do it well! Go make a difference!!

Stop being down because things aren't the way they used to be; you don't have the money you used to have; the figure you used to have; the relationships you used to have. Move forward in a positive, purposeful direction. Stop focusing on the past and focus on the present.

Sometimes, you just need to get out of your own way. You are trying to over-do and over-think! Relax a little, love!

What you THINK you see is not always what you REALLY see. You may notice a home filled with what looks like happy activity - a family playing in the yard, lights reflecting a warm and cozy glow. Everything may appear as if all is lovely and the occupants' lives are perfect. However, what you imagine may not be what is true. Realize that circumstances that "look perfect" may be wearing a disguise!

Tough times...They make us better if we allow them. It's easy to resent it when everyone around you seems like everything is perfect in their lives! But there are reasons for your trials. Besides, it could always be worse. So focus on all the good things! If you don't, you will simply crumble and that won't do anyone any good!

May you have new eyes to see the great purpose in your life! Believe your life exists for good reasons. Live according to the road map that leads to your purpose. Focus on this road map and don't stray from it! It will lead you to your destination.

What is a strong person? A person who endures through trials, stays positive, understands there is a greater purpose than merely what is seen, knows the power in the unseen, and seeks and trusts the higher source.

How are you impacting the lives of others (not even on a large scale but on a friends and family scale)? Leave a stamp on this world that says, "I was here!"

There are people who will call you a fool today and a hero tomorrow... Don't hesitate because of them... Keep going forward with your passion. Have COURAGE to do what is right.

Sometimes you are faced with making difficult decisions and choices. Making those decisions and choices knowing you may face consequences can be a tough pill to swallow. Knowing something has to change and making the effort to change makes you one TOUGH chick!

Don't be so stubborn, hard-headed, and prideful that you pretend everything is "okay" when it isn't. Sometimes you need to confide in someone you trust about your fears, shortcomings, insecurities and anxieties. Pretending everything is alright and not asking for guidance when you need it most is not healthy for your mind, body or soul. Let your guard down a little and see how much better you feel!

When you don't take care of things, you start a domino effect of problems. When you simply put a bandage over things and don't fix them right the first time, you are likely going to cost yourself more (more money, more heartache, more problems) in the end.

Don't forget people who have helped you get where you are. It can be easy to forget, but don't allow yourself to!

Friends are not just here to make you feel good but to make you think, to help you, and to guide you to make some changes if needed.

Don't pass up the opportunity to say you're sorry to your kids when you need to (when you've made a poor judgment call, haven't listened to their side all the way through, etc.). Apologizing shows them no one is perfect and sets the example for how to ask for forgiveness when they need to.

Give a smile to at least three people today. It's amazing how one smile from one person can change someone's day. Maybe someone will, in turn, think to give you a smile when you need one!

It's hard to walk with your chin up when your heart is heavy, but do your best, sunshine. It WILL get better!

In difficult situations ask yourself, "What am I not seeing clearly?" Step out of your shoes and try to see yourself from someone else's point of view. What do you see? Things you could adjust, things you could work on? If so, set some goals to make changes. There is ALWAYS room for change if you allow it.

Embrace life lessons believing they are merely like lights down the runway of an airport landing strip: There to guide you, direct you and keep you safe!

Take a good, hard look at things you are complaining about. Are they really problems??? Compare it to what someone else is going through... Do you need to rethink your complaints? Do you need to let them go? Do you need to adjust your attitude? Sometimes we get all wrapped up, stressed out and consumed by things that really aren't a big deal in the greater scheme of life. No one is saying the challenges you face aren't valid. But if you feel stressed out and overwhelmed, be encouraged to REALLY look at what you are facing. How relevant is it??? It may be very relevant... but open your mind and think it through before you allow it to affect your attitude, sunshine!

Believe your life is for a great purpose. Keep getting back up each time you feel as if you've been knocked down. There is a reason, a purpose for your life...keep going, sunshine. You just have to... PERIOD!

Are you fulfilling your passion and talent? If not, perhaps that's why you feel frustrated. Pay close attention to the pull of your heart and what you desire to do. You may think, "I can't do what I love. There's no way to do that at this point in my life." Start anyway! Whether it's a small baby step or a giant leap, it's amazing how things can work out if you follow the pull on your heart strings! But YOU have to make a move. When you know you are following the passion placed within you, you will find true peace. Passion and peace are things that can never be purchased with the dollar bill!

Go spend time with one of your girlfriends today! It is amazing how wonderful you feel after you've had girl time. Connection with other women fills your emotional tank and we function better when that need is met. We can be down in the dumps and a chat on the phone, an exchange of emails or going out to lunch with them turns us around. Our friends understand us, love us and guide us...we NEED each other!!!

Your personality can carry you much further than your knowledge sometimes. Your personality and your ability to have good people skills can overcome a lot!

You can't control the length of your life; however, you can control its depth!

You don't know whether to laugh or cry!!! You are completely overwhelmed in every area of life. You just want a break! There are so many of us walking around with smiles on our faces and holes in our hearts. Females need to be EMOTIONALLY charged, that's why we HAVE to have our "girlfriend time." We do so much in so many areas; however, we leave out one thing that is SO important...US time! You must be full to fill others up! Take time for yourself!

The attitude you embrace is more important than the circumstances you will face.

The power of real GF love is one of life's greatest gifts. It and your true GFs are always there when you need them!

You don't have to be rich to experience richness.

Sometimes you have to work for nothing to get something!

Be okay that some people are placed in your path for merely a season; learn from them, experience them and move on if it's necessary. Be okay with that.

Work like you don't need the money and love like you've never been hurt; give like your bank account is full and travel as if the world is yours for the seeing!

What if you stopped trying to control every detail and just let things flow? How much easier would your life be? Enjoy TODAY! Look for three positives today and write them down (there is something amazing about doing this!). You will usually end up with way more than three and you will see lovely things about your life even if you are in the "valleys" of life. Remember everything doesn't have to be perfect...to be perfect.

The more you think about GOOD things the better your life will seem. Purposely EXPECT good things to happen in your life. Positive Minds Produce Positive Lives!

When you have $$$ you have friends…when you don't have $$$ it's interesting to see who your friends really are!

Be your best! Live confidently in your strengths and talents! STOP comparing yourself to others… We each have gifts that are unique. Learn to be comfortable in your own skin, to focus on your inner beauty (which in turn makes true outward beauty). Feel good about yourself - YOU ARE IMPORTANT!!!

My mother-in-love (that is what I call my husband's mother) was guiding me through some hard times a few years back. She quietly listened to me and then she looked me in the eye and said, "Sweetie, you are BONAFIDE!" Ever since then she reminds me of this in emails, cards and phone calls. So I'm passing it along to you today: "SWEETIE, YOU ARE BONAFIDE!!!" This means that you are 100%, authentically YOU! Life is tough sometimes - staying true to yourself will give you the assurance that you are doing a good job.

Confidence: The feeling you have just before you understand the situation.

When someone is "taking shots" at you, disappointing you, or letting you down... Do not stoop to their level. Don't let your emotions control you; instead, you control your emotions! STAY CLASSY, sunshine!

When in doubt, know your way out!

Stop being so hard on yourself! There are so many areas in which we are trying to succeed and it can be overwhelming! It is good to strive to do your best but not if it makes us stressed, short fused and grumpy! Focus on BALANCE! If you can't get it all done then perhaps you are trying to do too much!

BE FUN!!! Don't take everything so seriously; let the dust bunnies, laundry, and dishes pile up for an extra day. They aren't going anywhere - they will be there when you get back! Be that fun, excited, carefree person you KNOW you are - even if it's just for today... Go PLAY! Your spouse, children, and friends won't look back and remember how clean your house was today...They will look back and say, "THAT WAS A BLAST!" Go create a memory today, sunshine!! You WILL be okay... You WILL make it through... You know why? Because you don't have a choice...The sun will rise again tomorrow and life will carry on!

Sometimes you have to take a long, hard look at yourself and adjust some things. Look back at old videos and pictures to see how far you've come, how things have changed. It's easy to forget. Is what was important to you then really that important to you now? There may even be something that you wanted back then that you're happy now didn't happen for you.

Money cannot buy anything that will fill the hole we walk around with sometimes. You fill that hole by really listening to your inner voice within your soul. If you really obey it, really follow its pull, pay attention to where it leads you, complete the passion it places within... that large hole you feel WILL get smaller.

Sometimes you feel so raw...however, love, remember there IS an end to EVERY adversity.
You cannot live looking back...so STOP dwelling on mistakes, missed opportunities, bad decisions, etc. This does you no good. When the past pops up in your mind, decide to move from the thought right then and there... Don't let it go any further!

Process your thoughts in the same way you use caller ID: some calls you answer, some you let go to voice mail and some you decline.

1-"I'll dwell on that thought because it does me good!" (Answer)

2-"I'll think about that thought when I can really digest it." (Voice mail)

3-" I won't think about that thought another second because it does me NO GOOD!" (Decline)

You've got to try hard to keep yourself out of the negative/blues "hole." EVERYONE has to fight it for one reason or another! No one has it all...so NEVER EVER feel like you are alone! You are not! It WILL be okay, you WILL get through!

In this game of life you have to use MENTAL strategy! You've got to keep your mind right each and every day so you don't fall into a pit. Be careful what you tell yourself, catch yourself in what you are pondering over, dwelling on. Think clearly at all times so life doesn't get the best of you, but instead, you get the best of life!

Life is definitely not the fairy tale story, but you will certainly get out of it what you put into it! Put some GOODNESS in your life today, sunshine!

When you are desperate you do desperate things... BE CAREFUL!!!

Your weaknesses, struggles and challenges end up being tools you can use to learn about yourself. And they can guide you in helping others who are going through similar situations. Instead of wallowing in feeling like "poor pitiful me," go help someone else! When you give of yourself to others, you not only help them but you help yourself as well. Sorry, no pity party for you today, love!

Displaying confidence, willingness, and positive action during difficult times is called 'COURAGE.' The way we react to situations speaks volumes about our characters.

It's amazing how one hurtful comment, one harsh look, one wrong attitude can affect our whole day! Why do we allow someone else that much power and influence over us? No one can MAKE us feel bad; only we can allow someone to make us feel bad. Even though it can be hard, consciously choose not to let someone else control our day, affect our smile, or take away the spring in our step! We control our happiness "volume," no one else does.

Trials, obstacles, temptations - they can all make you better if you choose to let them by using them in the right way. They not only build your strength, but they test and define the fiber of your character! For every trial you endure, every obstacle you overcome, every temptation you conquer, you become a superior soul, my dear!

Choose to invest in yourself in various ways...you'll look back and be thankful you did!

DO NOT focus on your fears and frustrations or they will captivate you. Focus on your hopes, dreams, what makes your heart POUND (your passion).

Stop thinking about what you have done, what you could have done or should have done. Learn from these things!

Concern yourself with what IS still possible for you to do. Move FORWARD, sunshine, even if it's one baby step at a time.

Too much of anything isn't always good.

Sometimes we have to do things we don't want to do, to be able to do the things we LOVE to do. If we keep this in perspective, it will help us to accomplish the dreaded deeds of the day.

Stay focused on what pulls at your heart ... Live your life with passion no matter what, sunshine!

Stay true to you!

You don't have to have everything to have EVERYTHING!!
Everything doesn't have to be perfect to be perfect!!

Dig down deeper and do what others won't.

My grandmother wisely said, "You never know if this may be the best of times; you won't know until you don't have it any longer."

Sometimes you've gotta "retreat" in order to move forward!

Live life with intent...If you do, your life will become miraculous!

Find the YOU you've been missing!!!

Don't forget who you are, where you came from, how hard you've worked and how much you are loved!

You ARE what you FOCUS on.

You have to believe you're great before others will believe it.

Challenge yourself, think outside the box, go for it...By practicing these things, you build your inner strength.

The older we get the less we tend to want more STUFF and the more we want more MOMENTS!

YOU CAN, YOU MUST and YOU WILL!

Don't do or say anything online you wouldn't do or say in person.

To achieve the possible you have to start with the necessary.

Use things and love people, don't love things and use people.

Do not concern yourself one more minute with people who attempt to tear you down. Move on from them and surround yourself instead with people with whom you can spend quality time, who know your true heart, who believe in you, who lift you up, and who know the REAL you! Keep being YOU!

You know WHO you are and WHAT you are all about…and the people who truly love you do as well!

Everyone has their moments.

Sometimes the ugliest, messiest, roughest times in your life are when your strength, endurance and determination are revealed. Dark times can bring deep understanding of important truths and clear vision IF you choose to allow it!

Do the best you know how to the best of your abilities!

May you be like the sun and reflect a warm, golden glow!

Remember ya gotta MOW what you SOW!

We have so many little things that we have to get done that can lead us to frustration! Our fuses become short and we EXPLODE! We keep adding things to our "to do" list that we could potentially eliminate. If you can't get it all done, perhaps you are trying to do too much. Evaluate and eliminate! Then BALANCE, ORGANIZE, PRIORITIZE and do not COMPROMISE on those choices!

Don't let people, situations or circumstance keep you in bondage! Get up and GO even when you don't feel like it because someone or something is holding you back!

Through the fire our weaknesses become our strengths. You don't have to go through one trial alone! Remember, there's no victory without a fight! You will be provided with the strength you need just when you need it! That's a promise, sunshine!

Don't waste your talents because you feel afraid, vulnerable or scared! Take a chance - you never know what may happen! You were given that ability for a reason. It would be a shame if you didn't utilize your gift....Whatever it may be (it could even be what you've been through that you could relate with others, a weakness you've overcome, etc, - not just singing, being an artist, a dancer, etc.).

Sweetie, you are MORE than that…Rise above it!!!

When you have a dysfunctional upbringing you end up trying to create a perfect world. Trying to keep your world perfect is eventually going to make you EXPLODE. Try to balance as much as you can. Everything doesn't have to be perfect to be perfect!

May you live today with a feeling that you have the strength to endure any challenge. May this moment inspire you. May you receive a new confidence that propels you forward!

You must deal with your issues down at the ROOT of the problem. You may have to discover (if you don't already know) where it's all coming from. If not, you will never be able to have complete peace. You should dig down deep and really discover the underlying cause then pull it out at the root! If you don't the effects will return and/or continue. Just like pulling a weed out of the ground...If you don't pull the WHOLE thing out by its ROOT, it will RETURN! Stop mowing the weeds! You will find peace this way.

A real friend doesn't have requirements! It doesn't matter how long you've been apart or what you did or didn't do for them. You simply pick up right where you left off!

When you are in the process of healing from something
the hardest part may be over. It's harder to be IN it than
to look back over it. You are already OUT of the situation
and now you are dealing with the effects of the wound. The
idea is to take GOOD care of that wound so it won't leave
a deep scar. If you ARE in the hurtful times (the actual
"wounding") please don't be timid about seeking professional
guidance. You must do the work to heal and grow from
your hurts. Take care of yourself in EVERY WAY!

Times are hard (emotionally, spiritually and physically).
People say they understand but they don't feel what you
feel. You won't be failed, dear! Your tears are seen and
your heart is felt. HOLD ON, help is on the way! Yes, it's
hard...But lift your head...Stay strong!

Men's minds are like the Christmas box with nice little dividers that holds the ornaments. They compartmentalize issues. Women's minds are like a box of lights all tangled up. It all blends together and never stops! Understanding the difference will help in dissecting issues you are dealing with.

Knowing what not to say is as important as knowing just what to say!

We are not confined in life by our environment, heredity, events that have taken place. We are free to seek and find a new way, new solutions and a new life! SEEK and FIND... elementary words that bring a PhD in life!

Are you allowing situations you are dealing with to rule your life? We all question certain circumstances and things we don't understand. Many times trials and challenges weaken you, blur your vision, make you weary and worn out! That's when frustration and discouragement creep in and take over. Remember that circumstances can change like the wind, so you cannot allow them to control your happiness! Joy is the one thing no one can take from you! It's not up for grabs! No deal!

Worrying cannot change the past! Worrying cannot control the future! STOP WORRYING, LOVE!

You don't know what you would do until you are personally in a situation! Forget what people may say! They probably don't have a clue what it's REALLY like in your world. Likewise, don't judge others' decisions! You just don't know until you've really been in those trenches yourself! Yes, it's hard to soar when you have broken wings. Sunshine, this is simply a season in your life. Tomorrow is a new day full of new promises, new hopes and new possibilities. You are loved! You matter! Someone cares!

When a new highway is built they have to cut down trees, dig down, remove soil, etc... They have to remove obstacles in the path to pave an easier way to a destination! There are seasons when obstacles are being removed to make an easier way for YOU! Just like the preparation for highway construction, it takes time to remove those obstacles. Be patient, sunshine - the "soil of adversity" takes time to be removed! However, as a result it will become easier to reach your destination!

Broken, bruised, and burned out? Trying to do it all? Sometimes trying to do it all makes you end up going in the opposite direction. You end up short-fused with the people you love the most! Perhaps it's time to restore, to rest and to rejuvenate...Slow down. Think about the issues you are dealing with...Will they matter a month from now? A year from now? If not, put them in their place!!! We want people to remember we had time and patience, that we cared for and listened to them - not that we tried to be a Super Woman. In the end, what really matters? Yes, we must get things done... But we just need to stay focused on what really matters: PEOPLE!

During a drought the roots of trees must grow deeper into the soil to find nutrients. Remember in times of trials to allow your roots to grow deep. Like the tree, it makes you stronger and more able to endure. No one enjoys a trial, but if you are open to being molded during this time you will look back and see how you have grown. We don't live forever, so create something that will!

Find the GOOD in the bad! Yes, it's very hard but it is there. All things work together like the pieces of a puzzle to create the complete picture.

There are so many beautiful things here on earth... and YOU are definitely one of them, sunshine!

About the Author

Jo Ann Darby is a Certified Personal Trainer (AFAA), Licensed Medical Esthetician, and North Carolina Esthetics Educator. She has worked as a Fitness Consultant for the Teen Tone Extreme Workout Video (Four Crossings Entertainment), as well as a Featured Model in *Muscle Media Magazine.*

Jo Ann currently owns Lake Norman Skin Studio Medi-Spa in Cornelius, NC. She has been married to her husband, Allen, for 19 years, with whom she has a son, Trevor (14) and a daughter and "Girlfriend," Alana (12).

The Girlfriend Book

MGFL or Much Girlfriend Love is the sister book to The Girlfriend Book.

The Girlfriend Book started as a mother-to–daughter journal when the author's daughter, Alana, was four years old.

Over the past seven years, Jo Ann Darby gradually added to her collection of practical 'every day' advice for her daughter, culminating in a body of work now known as The Girlfriend Book.

The Girlfriend Book was awarded finalist in the Women's Issues category from the 2011 Next Generation Indie Book Awards.

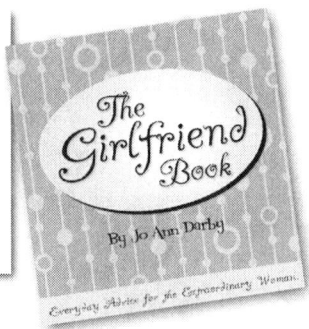

CPSIA information can be obtained at www.ICGtesting.com
Printed in the USA
BVOW081609111212

307872BV00008B/177/P

9 781886 057654